Lost and Found

LOST AND FOUND

Poems by
Andrew Merton

Accents Publishing • Lexington, Kentucky • 2016

Copyright © 2016 by Andrew Merton
All rights reserved

Printed in the United States of America

Accents Publishing
Editor: Katerina Stoykova-Klemer
Cover Photo: Gaspard-Félix Tournachon, self-portrait c. 1863

Library of Congress Control Number: 2015953127
ISBN: 978-1-936628-40-7
First Edition

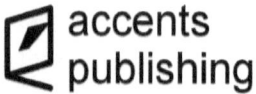

Accents Publishing is an independent press for brilliant voices. For a catalog of current and upcoming titles, please visit us on the Web at

www.accents-publishing.com

CONTENTS

I.

Being Andrew Merton / 3
Notes on a Progressive Education / 4
Crabbing / 5
The Day I Crossed Over to the Dark Side / 6
On a Dock in Mexico / 7
Apogee / 8
Of Moose and Seuss / 9

II.

On the Way to a Dylan Thomas Reading / 15
Showers / 16
Fifth Grade Air Raid Drill, 1955 / 17
Percussion / 18
Detroit / 19
Timing / 20
In the Woods / 21

III.

Validation / 25
Relic / 26
My Worth / 27
At Your Father's Place / 28
Your First Wife's Garden at Midnight / 29
Life After Dying / 30
Jehovah's Witnesses / 31
The Apprentice / 32

IV.

The Interrogation / 35
Honey / 36
Lost and Found / 37
Error / 38
This Music / 39
Anniversary / 40

V.

Discovery / 45
Yukon Go Home Again / 46
Bait / 47
Bear / 48
Man and Muskrat / 49
Heat / 50
What He Said / 51
Across the Street from Graceland: A Professor's Epiphany / 52
New Year's Eve on the Redeye from Logan to Heathrow / 53
Lesson / 54

VI.

Invasive Procedure / 57
General Anesthesia / 58
Chemo / 59
Addict / 60
Perspective / 61
A Fleeting Dream of My Sister / 62
Dark Grey Matter / 63
A Monologue and a Dialogue / 64
Grave Condition / 65
On the Last Night of the War / 66

VII.

Shorts / 69
Downpour / 70
On Any Given Day / 71
The Joys of Liver / 72
A Man of a Certain Age / 73
The Gift Shop / 74
Turkey / 75
Wrecks / 76
Prudence / 77
Fade to Black / 78

Survival / 79
Autopsy / 80
Biopic / 81

Acknowledgments / 83

About the Author / 85

For Gail, Gabe, and Rachel

I.

BEING ANDREW MERTON

Over a brandy my mother told me about the first boy,
stillborn two years before I came along:

how much she and my father had wanted that child.
How, for a month, they could not speak to each other,

even look at each other, without tears.
How it took them a year to try again,

and how, later, I was given his name.
She had not meant to tell me, ever—

It just slipped out, she said. *I'm sorry.*
She need not have apologized.

I would have taken the job
even had I known

I was not their first choice.

NOTES ON A PROGRESSIVE EDUCATION

1.

On a rainy day a teacher said
"Draw rain."
Through a window the boy saw streaks of grey
slashing toward the street.
These he reproduced.
The teacher shook her head.
"Where are the buildings and sidewalks
and people with umbrellas?
And that's not rain."
With a blue crayon
she drew a perfect drop.

2.

The children knew about the observation room.
From their side
the one-way glass
was a window to a night without stars.
Sometimes, as instructed,
they forgot about it,
but then it would call attention to itself
with the sound of a chair scraping the floor.
Once, a boy took a crayon
and drew on the glass
the face of a weeping child.

CRABBING
(Westport, Connecticut, 1948)

I tire of the heat.
While Father's back is turned
I slip over the side, quiet as a fish.

The current takes me away and down
past the bloody mackerel head
at the end of Father's line.

The river soothes me.
I scuttle sideways through the eelgrass,
breathing sweet, salty water.

Overhead, the shimmering moon of a sun
leads me on toward home
until my father's body blocks it out.

THE DAY I CROSSED OVER TO THE DARK SIDE

My friend Peter and I were six.
We wore cowboy hats, sheriff's badges,

and holsters with cap pistols in them.
We pretended we were at the top of a cliff

in the Badlands
(because they're full of bad guys, Peter said)

waiting to ambush some train robbers.
We must be a thousand feet high, said Peter,

from here those people down there look like ants.
There were three possible responses to this:

—They sure do.
—Those *are* ants.

—(I said): None of my aunts looks like that.
Sensing a change in me, Peter made new friends.

ON A DOCK IN MEXICO

The marlin hanging from a scale
is the center of attention,
like a birthday child.

My mother smiles at the camera.
My father smiles at the fish.
I am not in the picture.

On the day it is taken
I am busy turning five
in New York.

APOGEE
(Westport, Connecticut, 1951)

My mother snaps the photo: my father,
one foot on the bumper of his Buick,
leaning on a nonexistent rifle,

Hemingway with a rhino.
The war six years past,
his business is thriving, his heart still sound.

Later, wind gusts while he's burning brush.
The flames slither toward our house.
He sprays them with the garden hose, beats them with a shovel,

but they elude him.
My mother calls the fire department.
Our neighbors appear, and so, too,

do two shining hook-and-ladders.
Father backs the Buick away.
The firemen move with hunters' grace.

Soon the fire is out, the neighbors gone.
Father crosses the smoldering lawn,
dying embers in his eyes.

OF MOOSE AND SEUSS

In memory of Theodor Seuss Geisel, Dr. Seuss (1904-1991)

Down in old New York City, the Lower West Side,
Lived a small boy who sat in his room, where he cried
Because first grade was boring, upsetting, depressing;
The teacher, Miss Clamrake, believed in repressing
All notions of jollity, pleasure, or fun
Just after, or even before they'd begun.
Her style was pedantic, her demeanor inane,
Her idea of literature, Dick and Jane.
Dick and Jane! Those innocuous, vacuous twits
Walking here, running there, with no semblance of wits.
And that little dog Spot, with nary a flea,
Who must have been metal, wound up with a key.
The small boy, whose name, it is rumored, was Andy,
Told his mom, "You can't bribe me with money, or candy.
First grade is a torture much worse than the rack.
You can say what you want, but I'm not going back."
But she patted his head, and wiped off his tears
And said, "In a matter of only 12 years
You'll think of Miss Clamrake with kindness, I'm sure."
Then she gave him his coat and showed him the door.
He wandered the city, not caring or knowing
Where he had been, or where he was going.
The plans he made then for the rest of his life
Had no place for home or a job or a wife.
"The world of grown-ups is so dull I can't stand it,"
He said, "so I think I'll find work as a bandit.
An outlaw, a robber, I know I'll do fine.
I'll live a long life, and I'll die when I'm nine."
So saying, he stumbled and fell in the gutter
Where he continued to grumble and mutter
Till he noticed, of all things, a book in the street

With a moose on the cover. Right there at his feet.
A new book. Not tattered. Someone must have dropped it.
The boy, in his new line of work, went and copped it.
The title was *Thidwick, The Big-Hearted Moose;*
The author, a fellow who called himself Seuss.
The boy started reading. The moose was top-heavy.
His kindness had led him to take on a bevy
Of spiders and squirrels, and foxes and bears,
And birds who were making a nest with his hairs.
The moose was infested, beast-ridden and bent
From the weight of his guests, who paid him no rent.
And on top of all that—there were hunters! With guns!
Chasing old Thidwick in twoses and ones!
The boy pitied Thidwick. He knew how it felt.
The burdens of childhood were raising a welt
On his own head, which ached just like Thidwick's thick cranium
In all kinds of weather—in shine and in rainium.
His mother had told him to clean up his room,
And his father, a businessman, sounded like doom
When he said, "Mind your manners! Brush your teeth and don't slouch!
And don't ever again eat your lunch on the couch!"
It seemed no one ever said "Thanks" or "Nice job."
Instead they all chorused, "Don't be such a slob!"
It was enough to drive any young boy to despair.
It wasn't polite and it sure wasn't fair.
In this frame of mind he continued the story.
And soon both the moose and the boy ceased to worry.
For Thidwick the way to avoid being dead
Was to wiggle those antlers until they were shed!
His burden was lifted. His burden was gone.
He started life over, just grazing the lawn.
The boy was astonished. He had feared the worst.

Instead he had learned nice moose *can finish first.*
He went on to school and endured Dick and Jane
With a smile in his heart and a scheme in his brain.
In the library he read about Horton the elephant
Whose plight, as I'm sure you can guess, he found relevant.
And *The 500 Hats of Bartholomew Cubbins*
The Lorax, and Yertle, who took such a drubbin'.
And everything else by the whimsical doctor,
That world-famous, first-nameless, master concoctor.
Now the boy is much older. He writes and he teaches.
He climbs in the hills and he swims at the beaches.
He reads the old books to his children who thought
He was doing it for them. Until he got caught
With tears in his eyes when he read them the story
of a moose—such a moose!—in his pride and his glory.
Yes the boy's all grown up. He's read Kafka and Proust.
But still, on occasion, he likes to get Seussed.

II.

ON THE WAY TO A DYLAN THOMAS READING
(New York, 1953)

She's forty, the least sexy number,
she tells her friend Mark.
They're walking down Eighth Avenue
in the thick twilight of the West Village.

He twirls ahead of her.
You're sexy, he says.

How would you know?

They're passing the women's prison.
From somewhere up there
a she-wolf whistles.

See? says Mark. That was for you.
And you've been married three times. That's sexy.
Your husband thinks you're sexy. He's sexy, you know.

But business trips to Akron. Twin beds.
He doesn't want the children to think we actually—

He plays the cello.

He mangles Bach.

Poor Bach.

Bach's dead. Poor me.
She switches to a Welsh brogue:
Now our Mr. Thomas, the dear, sweet rogue …

who, within weeks,
will go roughly into that good night,
and her husband will say such a shame.

SHOWERS
(Frankfurt, Germany)

My grandfather, half Jewish,
on the board of I.G. Farben,
following the family dictum:
assimilate. He calculates

how many generations it will take
to dilute the troublesome Semitic blood
to nearly nothing. A waste of time;
he neglects to factor in Hitler.

Meanwhile, Farben scientists report
promising results with gas pesticides,
and he wants to stay around for the payoff.
He is certain his friends will protect him

until all this blows over.
Then one of the friends calls him in,
shrugs, the new order,
his services no longer required,

his safety no longer assured.
Thus, eight years later,
the smoke of Jews blowing all over Europe,
my grandfather is on the phone

in his apartment in New York,
nagging the Super,
because there's never enough hot water
for a decent shower.

FIFTH GRADE AIR RAID DRILL, 1955

I tell Mr. Carter there's a crack in the ant farm,
but he has more important things to talk about today:

After the bomb, trees will wither, milk will glow.
You might live a year before the insects get you

but first you have to survive the blast.
Duck under your desks

and stick your heads between your knees.
I pretend to do as I'm told.

When he turns his back I crawl away
on six legs, triumphant.

PERCUSSION

One day in 1956 four of us were up in the tree house in my backyard, trying to make animal noises, except for Big Lenny, who said the word *roar* instead of roaring. This was just before he leaned back against a wall that wasn't there. I thought about the sound he made when he hit the ground—*thud* was wrong, there was no *t-h*. My second thought was that Big Lenny was dead, but after a minute he rolled over, stood up, shook himself like a wet dog, groaned a real groan, and went on to become a drummer.

DETROIT
(August, 1961)

The day after their 17th birthday the red-headed twins Frank and Eddie and their friend Salvatore leave Bethpage, Long Island, in Eddie's '52 Chevy, headed for Detroit, by which they mean Royal Oak. A girl from their neighborhood moved there not long ago. Barbara is sixteen now. Back when she was seven she had invited them to her bedroom for a show. The only prop was a cardboard box with EGG written on it in pink crayon. Playing the part of a cygnet, Barbara hatched from the box, naked, before her mother ran in with a blanket. When Barbara moved she said come visit. On the road the guys eat greasy cheeseburgers, sleep in a motel with dripping toilets, and tell each other they're having a great time. Late on the second afternoon they pull into town and meet Barbara at a milkshake place lit up by a forty-foot neon cactus. There are four girls with her. She explains: I told them the boys from New York were here.

TIMING
(Thursday, May 17, 1962)

My father said goodbye
to my sister and me,
kissed our mother,

and left for work as usual,
wearing a white dress shirt,
a blue and grey striped tie,

a grey herringbone suit,
and black wing-tipped shoes.
He said he would be home late,

maybe 7:30,
but instead he died at 4:15
according to his brother,

who brought us the news.
While my mother and sister wept
my uncle turned to me:

You're the man of the house now.
The line sounded rehearsed.
Still, in one respect,

the timing was good;
By then I had been
eighteen for almost a week.

IN THE WOODS

Walking through nearby woods
following my father's death
I came upon a pileated woodpecker

smashing its noble head
against the naked trunk
of a dead poplar

like some crazed drummer
firing off rim shots
one after another.

Then, after a while,
the bird flew off,
leaving the tree to me.

III.

VALIDATION

We park in a ravaged woodlot
where the moon shines cold on icy stumps.
We did not intend to come
here, but lacked the price
of a hotel room.

Solemn to a degree
befitting two virgins
unwilling to wait until spring,
we undress, discussing spontaneity
and mechanical details.
Then, by pretending
until it is much too late
that this is only a rehearsal,
we succeed, technically.

When I look up he is there,
a boy our age, peering
open-mouthed
through a window
like a scientist
whose work, until now,
has been mere preparation
for this moment.
You scream, and he runs,
long before it occurs to either one of us
to thank him.

RELIC
(Maine, Winter, 1965)

Two o'clock Sunday morning.
Sleet outside,
and just one couple dancing

on a creaky frat house floor.
The place stinks of stale beer,
yet sounds still swarm like hornets

from the lead guitarist's amp.
His right hand's a blur,
a hummingbird's wing.

Staring at the ceiling,
seeing nothing,
he has the look of someone saved.

His bandmates want to get some sleep,
but what do they know?
They laughed when he told them

about his new pick,
the one he paid ten dollars for last week
to a man who *guaranteed*

that when that plane went down in Iowa,
they found this precious sliver
in Buddy Holly's hand.

MY WORTH
(circa 1968)

After not landing a job in Maine
I waited in a tiny airport
for a flight to Syracuse.
What had I accomplished in my 24 years?
Well, already I was laid off,
broke, divorced—that was something.
In a shack off the runway
an attendant weighed me on a cargo scale:
It's important to balance these small planes, she said.
Am I the only passenger, I wondered aloud,

as she walked ahead of me
out to a sixteen-seater
that resembled the remote-control toy
I had crashed as a kid.
I climbed in, feeling myself shrinking.
Sit there, she told me, fourth on the right,
which I did. What did it matter?
She left and returned with a large white box
which she strapped to the seat across from me.
Then she brought in seven more,

filling all the seats on the left side.
Have a nice flight, she said, and departed,
bolting the door from outside.
I thought I was alone,
until, from the boxes,
came scratching, scurrying sounds,
at which point I noticed the air holes.
By the time the plane took off
I knew I was, at least,
worth my weight in rats.

AT YOUR FATHER'S PLACE

Before we married,
before we fought

about fidelity, sex,
before the divorce,

your breakdown,
your death,

on a day hot as flesh
you took me to visit your father

who greeted us wet,
in his bathing suit,

gin and tonic in hand:
Cheers. Want to go skinny-dipping?

Your face cracked.
I should have known right then.

YOUR FIRST WIFE'S GARDEN AT MIDNIGHT

She's gone for good,
and you're out here with the spiders,

nearly blind,
thin as mist.

Overhead, the Crab Nebula
sucks away your shoes,

your music,
your old black dog

whose health gave out
with your marriage,

rips your grown-up coat right off your back,
leaving you small and lost

in Macy's,
lady's apparel,

a perfumed web of lace and silk,
your mother nowhere in sight.

LIFE AFTER DYING

> This is number three.... / Dying / Is an art, like everything else. / I do it exceptionally well.
>
> —Sylvia Plath, from "Lady Lazarus"

I do it poorly, so far,
only one effort
on a cold Thursday evening,

twenty-nine, divorced
again, my reasons to live
swirling like ashes in the wind.

I washed down half a bottle of Quaaludes
with some whiskey,
and passed out.

In the morning, when I answered the phone,
a friend said, just checking,
are you coming to the show with us tonight?

That's tomorrow, I said, but he said no,
it's tonight, Saturday.
I had died for thirty-six hours.

Wife number three came later,
even two children and some poems.
Lady L perfected her art in her kitchen,

number four.
As for me, I've come to realize
half empty isn't half bad.

JEHOVAH'S WITNESSES

Someone knocks
Sunday morning
at the ungodly hour of seven.
Hung over, I have no more sense
than to open the door.
Sunlight hisses in like a fumigant.
Two smooth-cheeked men
in blue suits, white shirts, black ties,
stand like mannequins
in an F.B.I. supply store window.
One preaches. The other sells pamphlets
and checks names on a clipboard.
They save souls
the way my mother saved tchotchkes.

I give them money.
They go away,
leaving me
the better of the bargain.

THE APPRENTICE

He apprentices himself to the dogwood tree in his front yard.
From June to August to September

it transforms itself
from green, to yellow, to brown,

while the apprentice bides his time.
Now, in the evenings,

dew settles in around the tree;
by mornings, the dew has crystallized.

The apprentice thinks nothing of it,
for the middle of the day remains yellow, warm,

timeless as saffron.
He plays in the grass

while morning and night close in on him
from above and below,

and the tree, stripped naked, finishes her work.
Then, one cold November night,

the tree shows the apprentice
how to hide from the wind,

but he, still bulky with summer,
takes the full force of the gale, and flees.

Yet the tree is patient,
and the bumbling apprentice perseveres.

There will be other lessons.

IV.

THE INTERROGATION

When I bring Gail home to meet my mother
Uncle Willie is there, unexpectedly,
high on schnapps, his face florid.
Soon enough he spits out,
Gail, do you believe in God?
He pronounces it Gott.
Willie's a German Jew who, it is said,
was compelled to do unspeakable things
while fighting with the French resistance.
After the war he bought a farm
in upstate New York, which reminded him
of the Rhine Valley. I have seen him
test the electric fence
by closing his fist around the wire
and grinning as his forearm
goes into spasm.   Gail's soul, too,
is mostly sinew. Raised in what she calls
a piranha tank, she left God,
along with the rest of her family,
at sixteen. Now, though, she hesitates.
Well, she says, probably not in the literal sense,
I mean creating the world in six days....
Willie's having none of this.
He leans in, shouts each word:
Gail! Do You Believe In Gott?
She looks at me, shrugs. No, she says.
Willie glares at her, slams his fist on the table:
Gute!

HONEY
(Delphi, 1977)

A honeymoon
before the wedding
is possible,
the Oracle implied,
and one evening
as we wandered among the ruins

of the temple of Aphrodite,
a cloud bank opened its vault
and out slid the full moon,
coating the mountains
with pale, pure honey.
Austere marble columns

stretched out to receive it.
You stretched too,
and drank it down,
that sweet light
glowing even now
in our children's eyes.

LOST AND FOUND

for Gabe and in memory of Christa McAuliffe, January 28, 1986

In winter
the big wooden box

in your school cafeteria
fills with boots, sweaters, sweatshirts,

hockey pucks, scarves,
and, on the day

they brought in a TV
so you and your friends

could watch a teacher
leave earth,

one small sky-blue mitten.

ERROR

At a restaurant we talked about airplane crashes
as though they were ballgames:
errors, hits, final scores.

I said, "That one in Boston, 1973.
A DC-9 hit the sea wall.
Fog and pilot error. Wasn't there a survivor,

at least for a week or so?"
No one could remember.
Later, serving coffee, our waitress said,

"Someone raped my sister. A man she trusted.
She got pregnant."
I started to say I'm sorry, but she held up her hand:

"I'm the only one she told.
She wanted to get rid of it.
Abortions were hard to come by then,

so I put her on a plane to Boston.
Two hours later, they pulled her out alive.
She hung on for more than a week.

Three whole months in fact.
I'm not asking much.
Just, next time get it right."

THIS MUSIC

for Rachel

I'm wearing my daughter's headphones.
I had meant to play Brahms'
Variations on a Theme by Haydn,

But it's Peggy Sue, Peggy Sue.
I'm fourteen again, short,
big feet, bad skin.

Peggy Sue got married
and Wendy Steiner won't go out with me.
Then she comes in, my daughter.

Grabs the headphones, boogies,
kisses my cheek.
Nice face, she says,

and she's gone.
This music.
It's enough to make you cry.

ANNIVERSARY

    for Gail

Tying the not.
That's how I heard it when I was a kid.
Later I thought of marriage as a rope,
not in a bad way,
just something that stretched on through life.
In my family, though, it mostly didn't.

We got married in our backyard, under the elm.
Your second, my third. (Wedding. My first elm.)
The omens stank.
It was hot,
you were sick,
and the well had run dry the day before.
By the time everybody left you were running a fever.
German measles.
We spent our wedding night
talking about old times.

There's a lot you can do with a rope.
Play tug o' war.
Hoist a piano. Ring a bell.
Hang yourself, or somebody else, or a swing
from an old elm tree.
Which somebody had.
My twelve-year-old nephew sat on it that afternoon
looking bored,
but he said later he'd been watching monarch butterflies
on their way to Brazil.

It's been thirty-five years.
Four of the guests are dead,
along with the elm.

My nephew learned Hebrew.
You and I had a new well drilled
six hundred feet into bedrock.
Then we had two children.
You, mostly,
but I cut the cords.

V.

DISCOVERY

Toward evening, near the river, I came upon
an ankle-length skirt, neatly folded,
two pairs of sandals,
and a wicker picnic basket
in which I found
two silver wedding rings
and, on the back side of a scrawled farewell,
a printed recipe for shepherd's pie
that turned out to be delicious.

YUKON GO HOME AGAIN

says the sign outside what used to be
the funkiest dive in the state.
After you left, it hit hard times.

The walls are puce, the ceiling's chartreuse
and a man in the corner sings the blues
in all the wrong hues—

robin's egg, sky blue, azure.
He was born too late to be B.B.,
and anyway, what can you expect

from a guy called Bradley
with a pink ukulele named Fred?
You're needed there to set things right.

Wearing faded jeans and hiking boots
and a low-cut flannel shirt,
you'll touch Brad's cheek

and reveal to him
that he's really a legend
named Old Blind Dog

with a guitar called Big Momma.
Then the blues will flow like midnight
in the roadhouse of your heart.

for Carrie Heimer, who returned to Alaska after a long absence

BAIT
(Rockland, Maine)

As the harbor wind shifts,
a stench like a wall of fish

slams into a couple from the city.
Tanned, elegant, eyes shaded,

they're as distant as manikins.
"Bait," says a local guy

who saw them wince.
There's a mermaid on his left arm,

an anchor on his right,
a cigar stub in his mouth.

Chest hair leaks over the top
of his whitish tee-shirt.

He points to an old steel ship:
"I used to work there.

She holds a ton of minnows.
I still like to come around

and watch them unload.
There's a special skill involved."

He winks. "Come on down with me.
I'll show you all the tricks."

The husband turns away.

BEAR

One morning a bear wandered through the yard.
They were fighting then, not about money or sex,

but about whether his shirt was green or blue.
You will call this a mere disagreement,

but on days when hate trumps love
green versus blue can be deadly,

and there is no place for teal.
The bear, black, three-quarters grown,

ignored the birdhouse but trampled the herb garden
before shambling off into the woods.

This was no shaman, no vortex,
no muscle-bound metaphor,

simply (to say just would be unjust) a bear,
but that was enough to change everything.

MAN AND MUSKRAT

In my dream I sit on the curb
of a busy street in Prague,
halfway between the castle on the hill
and Kafka's tiny house down below.

It was not always this way, I tell passersby,
pointing to my three-day beard, torn jacket,
and the talking muskrat by my side.
Until recently I was a normal man

dreaming normal dreams
of Ava Gardner, barefoot, posing against backdrops
of canyons, mountains, oceans, glens, lace curtains.
Then the muskrat arrived, speaking Czech,

which, I realized, I understood.
Do Prahy, it said—To Prague—and here we are.
Let me assure you, I have nothing against muskrats,
or Prague for that matter, but I miss Ava. Can you help?

But the muskrat says, ignore him,
and the passersby comply,
and later I awake, as I always do these days,
on a bed of water lilies in Bulgaria.

HEAT

Not long after your sister's house burns down
we rush out to see *The Merry Widow*,
although I would have preferred to stay home,

sit with you by the fire,
listen to Celtic music,
drink whiskey, wine,

make love.
Halfway through act one,
Anna and the count smoldering,

I remember a gas burner
I forgot to turn off.
We race home

to find the house cool.
You touch my shoulder
and go to bed.

I pour myself a shot of whiskey,
the cheap stuff,
the stuff that burns.

WHAT HE SAID
(at an art gallery opening in a gentrified seaside town)

Later, in the car,
he explained to his wife
that he was trying to say something nice
to the nice woman who ran the place.
Nice is a nasty word,
said his wife. He knew this.

The nice woman was refined and elegant,
something she made a point of,
a long, slow point,
while, out of politeness,
he drank her wine.
This town has come so far,
she said brightly
(another nasty word).
Boutiques, bistros,
antique shoppes
(the way she said it,
he knew she meant shoppes),
chamber music, art,
all in the last ten years.
Before that, it was a sailor's town,
nothing but tattoo parlors,
pawn shops,
bars, and bad porn.

He had nothing against this.
Still, what could he say
that would not sound as nasty as,
that's nice?
What he did say was,
I'm glad the porn's improved.

ACROSS THE STREET FROM GRACELAND A PROFESSOR'S EPIPHANY

You, who have not settled in to your title
after all these years,
you're in one of those shops

full of Elvis mugs,
Elvis jackets,
Elvis umbrellas,

Elvis shot glasses,
stuffed hound dogs
and pink Cadillacs,

and you're telling yourself you're above this
but you're lying, you want it all.
Outside there's a big karaoke tent

packed with sixty-year-olds
mangling In the Ghetto
and Cold Kentucky Rain.

You could do better,
you're a performer after all.
Then someone explains:

Those are amateurs up there.
The real impersonators are on a break,
and now you know who you are.

NEW YEAR'S EVE ON THE REDEYE FROM LOGAN TO HEATHROW
(or, The Fire This Year)

The big Englishman in the seat next to mine
says Jesus didn't need a plane to fly—
he soared like a falcon out of that tomb.
I reply that just now I'm busy designing a coffin
for the dying year. He ignores me and continues,
Jesus flitted around like a hummingbird for forty days
before ascending to his Father's side in Heaven.

Intrigued by Jesus's transformation from falcon
to hummingbird, I ask the Brit whether he's seen
the Angel of the North, near Newcastle just off the A1,
a twenty-meter torso with airplane wings,
a man and a plane and a cross rolled into one.
Bloody blasphemous thing, says my companion,
it ought to be melted down,
as Jesus would have done long ago.

Trying to be helpful I say a year is shaped
like a cross as well, or a man, if you think about it—
solstices at head and feet, with the equinoxes
stretched out to the sides like arms,
which I'll have to fold inward if I'm to
get this one in a box.

Somewhere over the ocean our pilot tells us
we've crossed into January. Decision time,
and I ditch the coffin plan.
Not that the past year was any worse than most;
still, best to prevent any hovering.
Cremation it will be.

LESSON

My lecture on the connection between the aesthetics of anarchy and the grammar of surrealism goes well until the Devil appears, unbidden, among my notes on the blackboard, wearing a tank top, tight denim cutoffs, and, on her left bicep, a tattoo of a satyr. She bears a remarkable resemblance to my high school crush, the elusive Julie. I am rendered briefly speechless before composing myself sufficiently to carry on, while, through it all, my placid students continue sipping their Molotov cocktails and rolling their eyes on the floor like so many lost marbles. Following class I flee. By the time I return, intent on erasure, all that remains on the board is a pink Maidenform bullet bra, unclasped at last.

VI.

INVASIVE PROCEDURE

While Albanians and Serbs
slaughter each other in Kosovo
I go in for surgery in Boston.
Just before putting me under,
the anesthesiologist, a young man
eager to put me at ease,
says cheerfully,
in an Eastern European accent
I cannot identify:
So. What do you think of the war?

GENERAL ANESTHESIA

You feel a pinch and away you go,
a small boy again,

whirling through that corridor you've read about,
all the way down to a joint called Heaven,

a worn ballroom on Seventh Avenue,
where it's still a dime a dance,

twelve for a dollar.
Your mother clasps you to her waist

and twirls you around,
her lilac-scented hair tickling your nose

while below you, long trains rumble
into a bright white station

where, soon enough,
black tiled letters will herald your arrival.

When you awake you'll remind yourself
that although there is no hurry,

if this is death, you'll take it.

CHEMO

in memory of Jane Pufky Nesbitt

In '65 David drove her east,
this secretary from Syracuse,
to meet his college buddies.
David in a Red Sox cap,
unveiling Jane like next year's Cadillac:
*She's smarter than all you jackasses combined.
Sexier too, and she makes more money.*
All of which was true: Jane, blonde,
deadly in a black ribbed sweater,
regarding her cigarette like Lauren Bacall.
Jane was a woman and David, well,

he seemed older.
He reads the paper to her now,
and cooks for her,
even lifts the spoon to her mouth
when she can't.
He says her Red Sox cap is sexy.
He does a bump-and-grind:
You can leave your hat on.
Jane smiles, closes her eyes.
Jackass, she says,
maybe in her sleep.

ADDICT

Once again I stand before the weary magistrate,
charged with possession of enough dark matter
to disturb the equilibrium of the universe.
As usual I have no memory of acquiring the stuff,
yet how can I deny it,
with night coursing through my veins,
the planet trembling beneath my feet?

PERSPECTIVE

Consider the good fortune
of the scrawny pigeon
on an icy sidewalk

outside a Boston movie house,
feasting on the contents
of a bag of popcorn

dropped there by my sister,
whose terminal illness
caused her hands to shake.

A FLEETING DREAM OF MY SISTER

In memory of Harriet Susan Webster (1947-2011)

You return from your Cape Ann Garden
where we scattered your ashes

and from my shoe tops
where some of that fine dust settled.

(I left it there for days,
like Elvis's autograph

on a teenage girl's hand.)
You return from the hospital

where nurses combed your fine hair
when there was nothing else left to do.

You return to Long Island, 1960,
where our parents roam the earth

as though they always will.
You ask me to drive you to school,

which I do, one last time,
much too fast.

DARK GREY MATTER

The
rate of
acceleration
of the expansion
of my incomprehension
of the nature of the Universe
turns out to be far greater than even
Stephen Hawking could ever have imagined.

A MONOLOGUE AND A DIALOGUE

After heart surgery
a doctor and a nurse stand by my bed.
The doctor tells me:
Everything went well.
We cauterized the areas
that were short-circuiting both atria,
causing the flutter on the right side,
the arrhythmia on the left.
You'll have to take it easy for a week
to allow the wounds
where we went in through the groin
to heal properly,
and we won't know for two months
whether we got everything
or whether you'll need a follow-up procedure,
but right now everything looks good.

The nurse says: How do you feel?
I say I really have to pee.

GRAVE CONDITION
(May 10, 1988)

We have your mother in the hospital,
says a nurse on the line from Long Island.
It's serious. You need to come down.

How serious?

I can't tell you that. It's confidential.

I'm her son.

I'm sorry I can't tell you more.
It's hospital policy.
You need to come down quickly.

It's a 300-mile drive from New Hampshire.
Is there any point in my doing eighty-five?

A pause.
No.

ON THE LAST NIGHT OF THE WAR

in a bombed-out city
on a deserted street,
a black dog crawled into our tent.
You clung to him
as you no longer clung to me;
this came as no surprise.
I walked away,
thinking peace was near.

VII.

SHORTS

Fourteen years after my mother's death
I'm in the old neighborhood,

walking through Washington Square Park,
when I see her from a distance,

sitting on a bench,
young again, slim,

her dark hair permed,
a string of pearls at her throat.

She's reading a book, hardcover,
Steinbeck's latest, I'm thinking,

or something by Daphne du Maurier.
There's a shopping bag from Gimbels at her feet.

I take a step in her direction.
Then she looks up, calls out,

and from another direction I come running,
five years old, wearing shorts.

DOWNPOUR
(Fifty years after my father's death)

Back then it took me a week to cry,
a year to stop.

Over time I got used to it,
in the way, I imagine,

a wounded soldier gets used to a bullet
lodged in his skull—

ignoring it as best I could,
working, marrying, drinking,

raising two kids,
not even minding much

when the old man's voice came out of my mouth.
Still, there are days like today

when I think about a woman I once saw
standing in her front yard, weeping,

garden hose in hand,
watering her lawn in the rain.

ON ANY GIVEN DAY

At a microphone behind home plate, the ghost of Eleanor Roosevelt belts out the Ode to Joy.

A butcher recoils from the smell of carrots.

A dark-haired beauty cites DNA evidence as proof that she is descended from Noah's raven.

A young nurse stops me on the street and asks me what I have done with the unicorn.

The State of Loneliness holds an election. The results are inconclusive.

The blood lust of the executioner's spare axe becomes unbearable.

I talk to trees. Most ignore me, but a stately pine tells me I'm nuts.

Grace spends a night in a tent in Maine. For miles around, moose are transformed.

Back home, the rhinoceros waits.

THE JOYS OF LIVER

Chicken livers fried,
calves' liver grilled,

best of all, my own,
just now marinating

in a savory solution
of malt, juniper,

and old vine wine,
as it will again tomorrow

and, given some restraint,
again and again

for decades to come,
regardless of wars,

earthquakes,
and paroxysms of the heart,

its crazy upstairs neighbor.
All I know is,

whoever named this organ
named it well.

A MAN OF A CERTAIN AGE

Some days are better than others.
Out walking today, for example,

he waves to a young woman from work.
Should he say something?

No, best to move on.
Over coffee last week,

seeing that her mouth was kissable,
he made a gentle suggestion

about a hidden meaning
in something she had said.

She blushed and smiled,
and it occurs to him now

that sometimes that's almost enough.

THE GIFT SHOP

An elderly woman seeks something, she says,
for herself, for having survived all this.

I show her the usual stuff,
the dark side of the moon,

the philosopher's stone,
the rainbow over Victoria Falls,

and everyone's favorite,
the Holy Grail.

To each of these she shakes her head.
She is a person of austere tastes, she explains.

In the end she leaves, content,
with a small wooden box

containing the answer
to the infuriating riddle of the walrus.

TURKEY

A wild turkey appears in my yard,
a fine fellow with a fiery red wattle.
Under the oak he spreads his tail feathers,

struts, looks around,
and wanders to another spot.
He displays himself three more times,

then disappears. As will I.
And then what will you say of me,
all of you, wife, children,

colleagues, students, friends?
He was a fine fellow.
Such a shame he was never fine enough

to suit himself.
A few decades left, at most.
Time to stop preening.

WRECKS

In my youth, I explored the rainforests of the Amazon,
taking equal delight in my observations
of piranhas, deadly bushmasters,
brown-skinned women, exotic birds.

Then an old man picked me up in his flatbed jeep.
I sat in a banged-up seat wedged into the rear.
The man told me he was driving in the jungle one day
when he came across the wreckage of a small plane,
the pilot long dead,
vines and snakes creeping through his eyeholes,
so the old man took the seat. He grinned:
That is why I can give you a ride.

Darkness approaches slowly.
Yet again tonight, at some dive in Maine,
with snow drifting outside,
the pilot rests a hand on my shoulder.
I order another double and share it with him.
It seems the least I can do.

PRUDENCE

Consider, for example,
the chickadees

who store seeds
from the feeder

in my front yard
in the rough bark

of a nearby oak,
a sensible hedge

against my inevitable negligence
or death.

FADE TO BLACK

Somewhere along the coast of Maine
two crows explore a ragged beach,

pausing now and then to bicker over
crabmeat, or tear apart a rotting fish.

I concede there have been other birds:
herons, sandpipers, cormorants,

frenzied gulls, and once a puffin,
blown in by some aberrant wind.

I found ways to love them all. Still,
as the tide ebbs and twilight closes in,

the crows remain.

SURVIVAL

In this game,
the object
is to finish
dead last.

AUTOPSY

When they cut into me they find

a black mongrel that can outrun a greyhound

my father's Steinway upright,
his yellowed score of the Moonlight Sonata
still open on the stand

an old rubber ball
lost in some dark corner
of Washington Square Park

the young Willie Mays,
sprinting toward the wall,
cap flying,
on black-and-white TV

a secret desire to be named Conway Twitty, Ferlin Husky,
or Mame

a python, a boa, a little black hole, and a slice of pi

Shere Khan

the Old Jewish Cemetery in Prague

the Callanish standing stones
on the Isle of Lewis at sunset

a red '54 Caddy convertible, top down,
with Dynaflow transmission

an empty bottle of Jameson's

and a needle from one of Monet's haystacks,
which they list as the cause of my death.

BIOPIC

At the end of the film of your B-list life
the A-list actress playing your young widow

walks away from your grave,
shrouded in black from head to foot:

veil, cloak, ankle-length skirt, stockings,
four-inch heels.

At the premiere she sits with your actual widow,
whose name appears in the credits

(where yours does not),
both women sheathed in crimson,

surveying the audience,
each contemplating her next role.

ACKNOWLEDGMENTS

Thanks to (clockwise, starting with you on the chair next to the piano) Mekeel McBride, Kendra Ford, Kimberly Cloutier Green, Shelley Girdner, and Jody Hetherington for their insightful criticism over the years, and to Katerina Stoykova-Klemer, who brings out the best in those of us who are fortunate enough to write for her.

The author is grateful to the editors of the literary publications in which the following poems first appeared:

"Being Andrew Merton": *Family Matters: Poems of Our Families,* Bottom Dog Press, 2005

"Of Moose and Seuss": *The Boston Sunday Globe,* October 6, 1991

"Fifth Grade Air Raid Drill, 1955": *Blast Furnace,* Vol. 4, Issue 1, 2014

"Percussion": *Vine Leaves Literary Journal,* Vol. 10, 2014

"Detroit," "The Interrogation": *The Louisville Review,* #77, Spring, 2015

"Validation": *Spillway,* #16, Summer, 2011

"Across the Street from Graceland: A Professor's Epiphany": *The Rialto,* #78, Autumn, 2013

"Chemo": *Hospital Drive,* forthcoming

"A Monologue and a Dialogue": *American Journal of Nursing,* June, 2015

"Downpour": *Driftwood Press,* #1, Winter, 2013

"Turkey": *Passager,* Summer, 2006

ABOUT THE AUTHOR

Andrew Merton is a journalist, essayist, and poet. Publications in which his nonfiction has appeared include *Esquire, Ms. Magazine, The New York Times Magazine, Boston Magazine,* and *The Boston Globe.* His book *Enemies of Choice: The Right-To-Life Movement and Its Threat to Abortion,* was published by Beacon Press in 1980. His poetry has appeared in *Bellevue Literary Review, Alaska Quarterly Review, The Rialto* (U.K.), *Comstock Review, Louisville Review, Vine Leaves,* the *American Journal of Nursing,* and elsewhere. His book of poetry, *Evidence that We Are Descended from Chairs,* with a foreword by Charles Simic (Accents Publishing, 2012) was named Outstanding Book of Poetry for 2013–2014 by the New Hampshire Writers' Project. He is a professor emeritus of English at the University of New Hampshire.

www.ingramcontent.com/pod-product-compliance
Lightning Source LLC
Chambersburg PA
CBHW021446080526
44588CB00009B/709